# stepping
# stones

WISDOM & ENCOURAGEMENT
FOR YOUR
PARENTING JOURNEY

## MARK
## GREGSTON

*"Dedicated to the kids at Heartlight....*

*you have taught me well."*

*Stepping Stones: Wisdom and Encouragement for your Parenting Journey*
Copyright 2011 by Mark Gregston
Published by The Heartligtht Ministries Foundation
P.O. 480
Hallsville, Texas 75650

# CONTENTS

RELATIONSHIP

*Your teens need a relationship with you more than anything else you could ever offer them.*

∽o∽

*A great way to build a relationship with your teenager is to find a challenge you both enjoy, and participate in it regularly.*

*A healthy relationship with your teenager*

*is founded on unconditional love.*

❧

*Disrespect is usually a symptom*

*of a deeper relational problem.*

*Do you take the time to connect with your teenager*

*only when things are going well?*

༄

*Have you made the commitment to stay engaged*

*in your relationship with your teen,*

*even when the going gets tough?*

*Wise parents show their teen they are as
interested in maintaining the relationship
as they are in enforcing rules.*

∽○∽

*Listening, and giving your teen a chance to speak,
communicates that he is valued and accepted.*

*Parents need to restore a relationship
with their teen before they can be effective
in correcting their teen.*

∽◦∾

*Relationship should never be
a bargaining tool with your teen.*

*Sometimes grace can break through*
*the walls of a broken relationship.*

∽○∾

*Grace is unwarranted forgiveness,*
*unilaterally applied.*

*Teens tend to be hyper-sensitive to relational problems*
*between their parents, even if the problems are*
*thought to be carefully hidden.*

∾∘∾

*You can expect good behavior,*
*but don't let your relationship suffer because of their mistakes.*

*You can't touch or see a sense of significance,*

*but that's what teens long for—*

*through a loving relationship with you.*

∽∞∽

*Show your teens how to have fun, to productively occupy*

*their free time, and to enjoy and celebrate an abundant life.*

*Kiss and hug your spouse in front of the kids.*
*Your marriage is the close-up-and-personal example of what*
*an intimate relationship looks, feels, and sounds like.*

∽◦∾

*You'll know your teen is maturing when they*
*seek your input and value your advice.*

*Serve and care for others and pass on the tradition to your teenager. Times volunteering or helping others as a family will instill character and build lasting memories.*

∽∾

*Acknowledging that you aren't perfect won't destroy your teen's high regard.*

*When your kids grow up, they won't remember if the house was perfectly neat and clean, but they will remember whether or not you spent time with them.*

∽∾

*A word of encouragement in the midst of failure is worth more than an hour of praise after success.*

*An ounce of prevention is spending time with
your teen on a regular basis rather than force-feeding
a pound of cure when issues arise.*

∽∾

*It's better to be a model of good behavior
than a critic of misbehavior.*

17

*Build an extended family for your teen,*
*made up of family or friends.*
*It will bring strength and self-esteem.*

∽o∽

*Favor a perfect refuge for your teenager,*
*versus a perfect house.*

*Draw the line on modesty,*

*but don't go crazy micro-managing the way your teen dresses.*

∽◦∾

*A strong family life during the teen years is no accident.*

*It takes hard work.*

*Have you had a one-to-one outing*

*with your teen this week?*

&

*If the lines of communication are not established*
*before a conflict, then the parent must first work*
*on that before attacking the issue.*

If a teenager shares what is on his or her heart,

and a parent misses it by not really listening,

then a teen will quit sharing altogether.

∾⌣∽

God will help you through

any problems with your teen.

*Notice the times and locations that your teen*

*is relaxed and willing to talk,*

*then seek out that venue for future talks.*

∾⌣∾

*Keep your promises to your kids and others.*

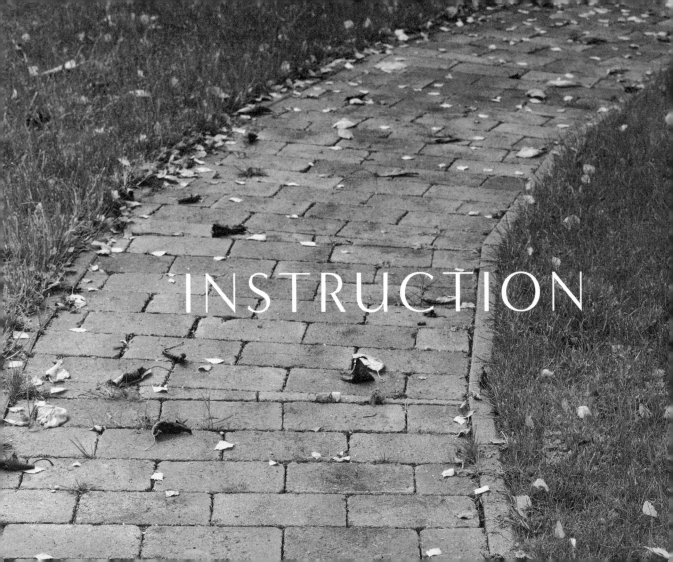

*Be assured that your teaching of values*

*has not fallen on deaf ears.*

~

*Discipline in the teen years should focus on*

*building positive character traits.*

*Don't expect institutions to*
*teach the basic rules of life to your teen.*

~

*"Parents can tell but never teach,*
*unless they practice what they preach."*
—Arnold Glasow

*Teach your teen that along with privileges*
*come responsibilities.*

❧

*Teach your teen that trust is a cherished commodity to be earned,*
*but also one that is easily damaged.*

26

*Praise your teenager's uniqueness.*

*That way, she won't feel pressured to be like everybody else.*

～

*Teach your teens that it's okay to cry,*

*but they shouldn't miss the opportunity to learn*

*from disappointments.*

*Teens can be easily fooled, so be sure to teach them*
*that if something seems too good to be true, it probably is.*

*"The most important thing that parents can*
*teach their children is how to get along without them."*
–FRANK A. CLARK

*What parents really need to teach their kids is as old as time:*

*the basic golden rules.*

~

*When watching a movie, discuss the moral issues with*

*your teen. Listen to their views, teaching them to*

*be discerning, not just accepting.*

*When your teen acts up, ask questions first.*

*His behavior may signal an issue or incident*

*you haven't heard about yet.*

❧

*When your teen feels overwhelmed,*

*teach them to focus on one thing at a time.*

30

*Teach that what other kids say about him or her*

*is just their opinion, not the truth.*

*You can teach your teenagers how to clean their rooms,*

*but your idea of clean and theirs may be different,*

*so praise them for the effort.*

31

*Let your teens know that failure is never final,*

*unless they give up.*

～

*Teach that while the easy way is to be lazy*

*and mess around in school, that often turns out*

*to be the hard way in the long run.*

*Remind teens that no one is perfect—*

*not you, not them, not anyone.*

⌒

*The art of conversation is an important social skill,*

*but parents often neglect to teach it.*

*Teach kids this trick: always notice the color of a person's eyes.*

—

*Making eye contact will help a hesitant teen appear more confident and will help any kid to be more assertive and less likely to be bullied.*

*Talk about the lessons to be learned*

*from other people's mistakes.*

*Be sure to teach your teenager your family's history—*

*both hardships and successes.*

*It builds esteem and stability.*

*Many teens will question—or shake free of—*

*some of the values you've taught in order to find their own.*

*Be your teen's spiritual mentor—*

*don't leave it up to your church or others.*

*The word mentor means a wise and trusted counselor.*

*"Children seldom misquote you. In fact, they usually repeat,*
*word for word, what you shouldn't have said."*

—AUTHOR UNKNOWN

~

*For teens, there is no better time to launch*

*a purposeful direction in life.*

*God uses people in your life, and just as iron sharpens iron,*

*He could be using your teen to sharpen you.*

*Show your teen how they can use*

*God's Word as their guidebook, prayer as their navigator,*

*and fellowship as their encouragement.*

instruction

Once a month take your teen

to explore some new activity, sport, or hobby.

It will reveal what you both enjoy together.

⟋⟍

How do you rate the job your parents did

when you were a teenager?

Is there something they could have done better?

39

*If you are sarcastic with your child,*

*then your child is likely to be sarcastic with you.*

~

*If you want your teenager to start asking questions,*

*go home this afternoon and don't say anything.*

*Kids sometimes temporarily abandon the values*
*they have been taught in order to find them again*
*and make those values their own.*

*Hold teens accountable to untangle their entanglements.*

One of the best places to have a discussion with your teenager

is when the two of you are in the car.

⁓

Pain is God's instrument to expose who we really are,

explain how life really is, and cause us to seek Him for answers.

Parenting a teen?

Stop lecturing and start listening.

~

Stop worrying and start praying.

Stop frowning and start laughing.

Share with your teen your own life mistakes and life lessons.

❧

Teenagers expect to be lectured, so why not try something new?
This time, just ask questions.

❧

Help your teenager by allowing him to help himself.

*With teens, don't share your opinion unless asked—*

*it keeps them thinking.*

~

*Your teen will do as you do, but not always as you say.*

*So set a good example.*

Let your teenagers see that you also have

shortcomings and setbacks.

This will help them be more realistic about themselves.

⁓

People live up to what you inspect, not necessarily what you expect.

So assure your teen you are going to be looking out for them.

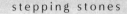

Say *"I love you"* to your teen whenever you feel like it,
even if it's 100 times a day. You simply cannot spoil
a teen with too many expressions of love.

———

Seek right things for the right reasons, confront with calmness,
and correct with firmness…all with a love
that seeks their best interest.

love

Remind your teens that there is nothing they can
do to make you love them more, and nothing they can do
to make you love them less.

———

Tell your teenagers, "I love you just the way you are."
The best way to handle extreme outbursts
is to answer their anger with love.

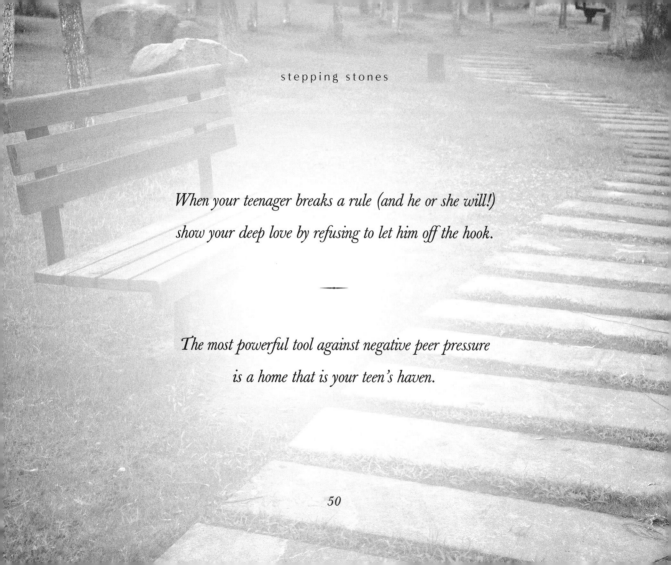

*When your teenager breaks a rule (and he or she will!)*

*show your deep love by refusing to let him off the hook.*

———

*The most powerful tool against negative peer pressure*

*is a home that is your teen's haven.*

50

love

*Be loving, even when you don't feel loving.*

——

*Don't base your love on your teen's performance.*

51

Don't tie love and acceptance to good behavior.

Let your teens know you will continue to love them,

regardless.

love

Don't burn bridges with a rebellious teen.

Instead, build them, fashioned after God's love and grace.

———

Say "I'm sorry" to your teens when you're wrong.

It teaches them to do the same.

*Don't put off until tomorrow what you can do today...*

*tell your teens you love them, whatever they do or say.*

———

*Your teen will gravitate toward whoever genuinely values him.*

*If not you, then he may find acceptance with the wrong crowd.*

love

*Don't compare your teenager to others.*

*Value her unique gifts.*

———

*God calls us to love our children in the midst of their sin,*

*so that we can be the one who is there to speak the truth.*

*Have you told your teen today that you love her?*

*Show your love by being kind.*

———

*Create a home where your teen finds rest,*

*not more ridicule and challenge.*

love

Give teens your undivided attention a few minutes every day,
constantly assuring them that they can always
express themselves freely.

———

Let your teenagers regularly "overhear" you praising them,
never "overhear" you cutting them down.

*The greatest gift you have to give your teenager is you.*

———

*The words that you say to your teen today*

*will stick with them throughout their life.*

*So make sure they remember some good ones.*

love

Unkind or ridiculing words can do lifelong damage.

———

If you've ever been verbally unkind in the heat of the moment,

ask for their forgiveness.

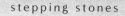

*We are never more like Christ than when we*
*choose to give our teen grace in the face of a struggle.*

———

*When teens misbehave, keep emotions under control.*
*Never allow anger to control your response.*
*If needed, step away before responding.*

love

When you know you've wronged your teen,
saying "I'm sorry" can calm the ripples your mistake
has created in your teen's life.

———

Whenever the boat (your home) is tossing and turning
In a sea of confusion and struggle,
your kids need to know what to grab on to.

61

*Be your teen's biggest fan.*

*Tell your teen, "My life is much better because you are here."*

———

*Be grateful for your family—problems and all.*

62

love

*Nothing happens by itself.*
*You have to work at having a good family life.*

———

*For one day, count how may times you criticize and praise*

*your teenagers. Work hard at criticizing less and praising more.*

*Pause and take stock of what really matters to you.*

*Put your time and energy there.*

———

*Family gatherings and rituals—such as dinners together, holidays,*

*and reunions—make a teenager feel more safe and secure.*

64

love

Look for improvements that you can praise—not just success.

If you are too busy to have fun with your teenagers,

you are too busy.

*Compliment your teenagers often in front of others,*
*and you will give them a reputation to live up to.*

———

*Your teen's behavior may be bad,*
*but that doesn't mean he or she is bad.*

love

*If you expect your teenager to be "perfect,"*

*you will always be disappointed.*

*They are just as human as you.*

———

*It is better to be a model than a critic.*

*Be specific with praise. It will mean more.*

———

*Notice times when your kids are most likely*
*to talk—at bedtime, before dinner, in the car—*
*and be fully available to listen.*

love

*When your teenagers are talking about concerns,*

*stop what you are doing and listen.*

*This shows them you care what is going in their life.*

———

*Listen to their point of view…*

*even when it's not what you want to hear.*

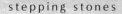

*Forget arguing about the small things*

*like fashion choices and occasional potty language.*

*Instead, focus on the things that really matter.*

———

*You are not your teen's friend. You are their parent.*

*Act like a parent and not a peer-ent.*

70

*Many parents spend so much time correcting their children*

*that they forget the greater need—connecting.*

———

*How you respond to your teen's stupid stunts is important.*

*Remember all the stunts you pulled as a teen before*

*you respond to your son, or daughter's.*

Realize that your teenagers may test you by revealing a small part
of what is bothering them. Listen carefully to what they say,
encourage them to talk, and they may share the rest of the story.

———

Affirm, affirm, and affirm.

DISCIPLINE

*Being a parent means handing out consequences*
*for misbehavior and offering plenty of love, acceptance,*
*and belonging at the same time.*

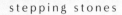

*Consequences are the result of a teen's decisions,*
*not a parent's desire to punish bad behavior.*

*Immaturity demands boundaries...*

*rebellion demands consequences.*

*Your goal is to help your kids get to where they want to go,*

*and keep them from where they don't want to go.*

*Even if they don't know which is which.*

75

*It's easier to put off consequences in favor of idle warnings,*

*but it leads to chaos in the home.*

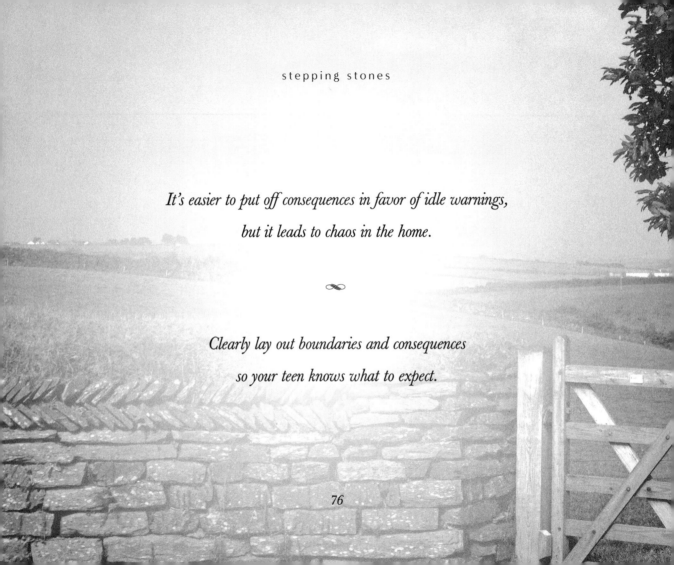

*Clearly lay out boundaries and consequences*

*so your teen knows what to expect.*

*Parents who allow their teen to suffer the consequences*
*of his mistakes tend to have a teen who makes fewer mistakes.*

*Parents can prevent future bad behavior in their teens*
*by establishing stronger consequences ahead of time.*

*Show your teenager that it is okay to be wrong,*

*to admit that you are wrong, and to learn from your mistakes.*

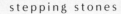

*Parents who are quick to correct with harsh words,*

*rather than allow consequences to do the correcting,*

*can damage a teenager's self-esteem.*

78

Rules and consequences that seem reactionary, arbitrary,
or inconsistent breed frustration and rebellion in teens.

There's nothing like knowing exactly what's in store
for a wrongdoing—so make the consequences clear.

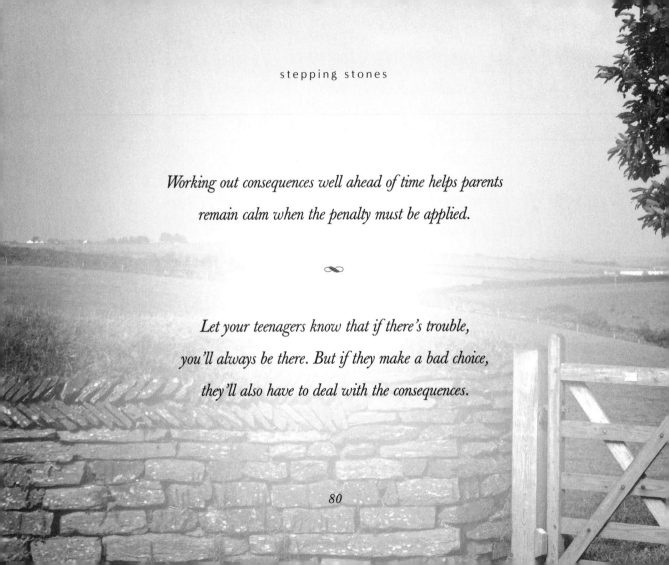

Working out consequences well ahead of time helps parents
remain calm when the penalty must be applied.

Let your teenagers know that if there's trouble,
you'll always be there. But if they make a bad choice,
they'll also have to deal with the consequences.

80

*Instead of coaxing your teenagers out of bed every morning,*

*buy them alarm clocks. If they're late,*

*let them deal with the consequences.*

*A wise way to train teens to behave responsibly*

*is to reward them when they get it right.*

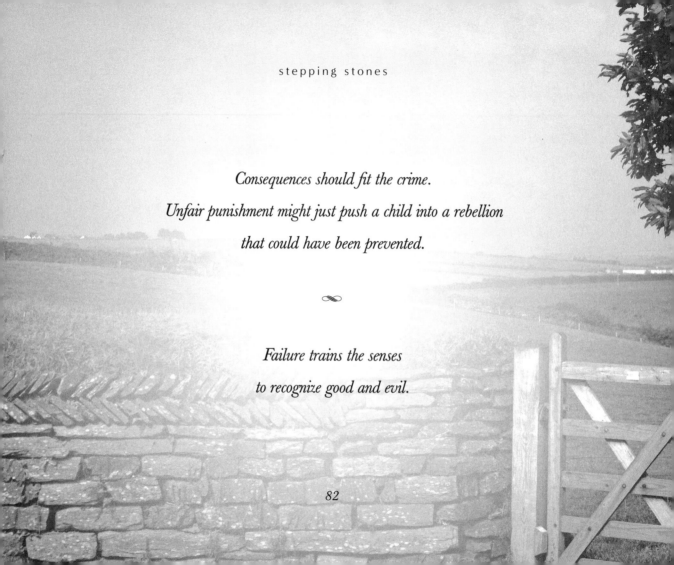

*Consequences should fit the crime.*

*Unfair punishment might just push a child into a rebellion*

*that could have been prevented.*

❧

*Failure trains the senses*

*to recognize good and evil.*

82

*Is it time to review the rules and boundaries in your home,*

*to determine if they need to be adjusted*

*to fit the maturity of your teenager?*

*Let your teen know that expanded privileges*

*will coincide with growing maturity and responsibility.*

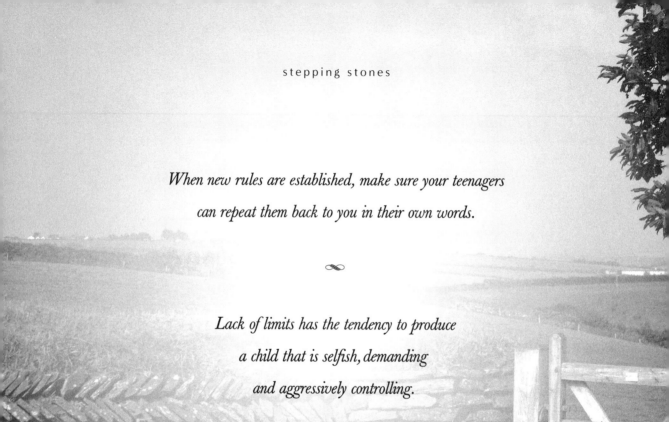

*When new rules are established, make sure your teenagers*
*can repeat them back to you in their own words.*

∞

*Lack of limits has the tendency to produce*
*a child that is selfish, demanding*
*and aggressively controlling.*

*Periodically talk to your teen about ways*
*for them to gain more freedom and independence.*

*Mom and Dad are in charge. That must be*
*the undisputed truth. Mocking or challenging*
*your authority should never be tolerated.*

85

*"Parents who are afraid to put their foot down usually have children who tread on their toes."*

—Chinese Proverb

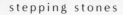

*Setting boundaries is good for teenagers. They will complain, but what they will feel is a sense of security and relief.*

*Remember, correcting your teenager isn't about you,*

*your reputation, or your parenting skills.*

*It is about helping them.*

*Teenagers cannot absorb too many rules without*

*giving up in exasperation. Focus your rules*

*on the things that really matter.*

87

*Self-control: not being controlled by the things*

*that have happened in your life.*

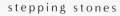

*Some parents fail to discipline their children for fear of becoming*

*like their own domineering parents. Enforcing rules and having*

*boundaries does not turn you into your parents.*

Sometimes a parent needs to allow other authorities

to introduce discipline into their teenager's life.

Teenagers fail to grow out of their childish self-centeredness

when every desire is fulfilled by their parents.

*Teenagers have an uncanny need for justice.*

*So, be a fair judge in your home.*

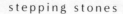

*The time your child may spend hating you is short compared*

*to the potential positive effect of discipline on their entire life.*

discipline

*Until the pain of your teen's bad action is greater than*

*the pleasure gained from the action, they won't change.*

∞

*When teenagers don't know what is expected in your home,*

*they will do what is right in their own eyes.*

*That is a recipe for disaster.*

Yes, set boundaries. Yes, stop enabling your child. Yes, know what
you believe and where you stand. But don't eliminate or reject
the one whom God has placed in your life for a reason.

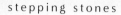

If the discipline you're using isn't working,
do something different.

92

Much teenage rebellion comes from treating them
like they are 10 when they are 15.

The key to changing a teen's unacceptable behavior
is to get to the root of the anger.

*I believe in consequences. But I believe they that they must be fair—*

*too bold of a stand might just push a child into*

*a rebellion that could have been prevented.*

*Consequences are a more effective teacher than your anger.*

LEARNING

*Engaging with your teen through the power of caring inquiry is crucial, but you must also learn to keep your mouth shut long enough to hear her answer.*

———

*Every responsibility you assume for your teen is one less learning opportunity for him.*

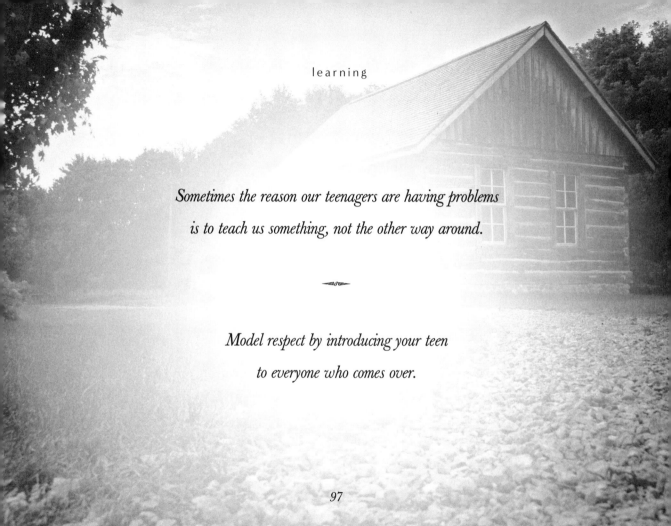

learning

*Sometimes the reason our teenagers are having problems*

*is to teach us something, not the other way around.*

*Model respect by introducing your teen*

*to everyone who comes over.*

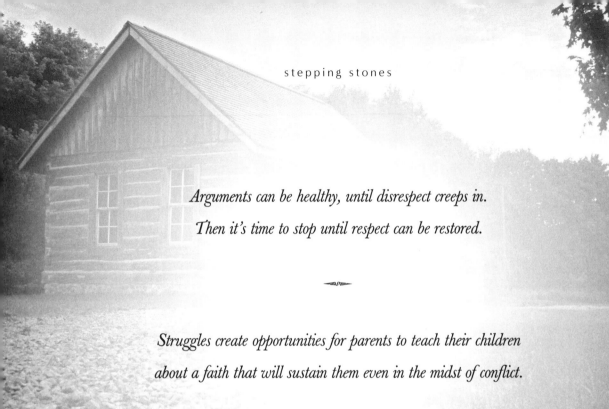

*Arguments can be healthy, until disrespect creeps in.*

*Then it's time to stop until respect can be restored.*

⸺⁖⸺

*Struggles create opportunities for parents to teach their children*

*about a faith that will sustain them even in the midst of conflict.*

*How parents fare when facing trials is a far better measure*

*of good parenting than whether a family struggles at all.*

*Learn to adjust your expectations about what you want*

*for your teen and what you want from your teen.*

*Tweak until neither you nor your teen is frustrated all the time.*

99

*Don't overprotect to the point that they miss out on experiencing*

*some great lessons necessary to function in the world.*

⎯⎯⎯

*Dialogue about values if you expect your teen to embrace values.*

*Thank your kids often for teaching you*
*how to be a really good parent.*

*The best way to teach your teen to be grateful is to be grateful*
*yourself, no matter what problems come up.*

*Faith can be learned by teenagers*
*who see it lived out in their parents.*

*Help your teens learn to forgive themselves*
*for the mistakes they have made.*

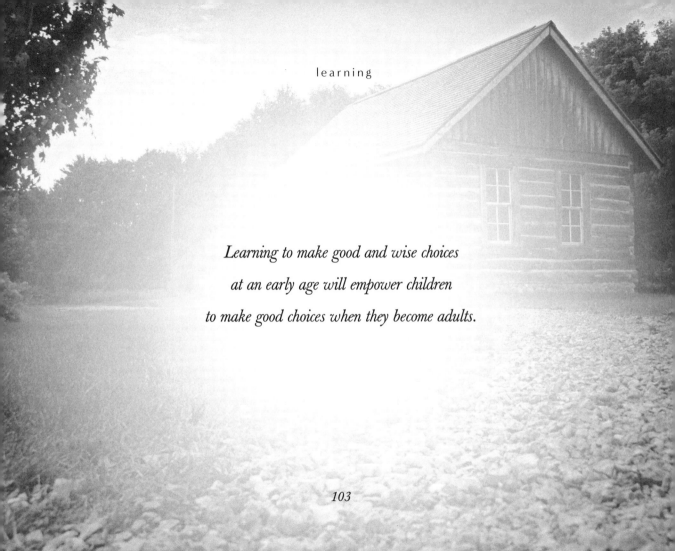

learning

*Learning to make good and wise choices*

*at an early age will empower children*

*to make good choices when they become adults.*

*Rules need to evolve over time as lessons are learned,*

*and be aligned with the growing maturity of your teenager.*

———

*Some parents shut off conflict with their teen.*

*Wise parents learn to manage it.*

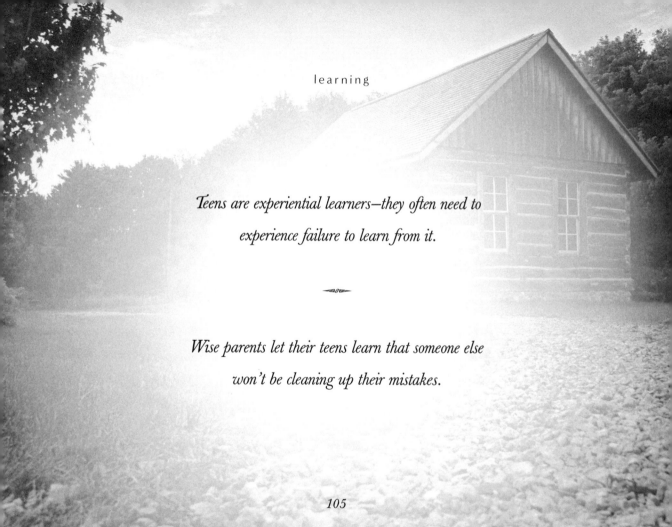

*Teens are experiential learners—they often need to experience failure to learn from it.*

*Wise parents let their teens learn that someone else won't be cleaning up their mistakes.*

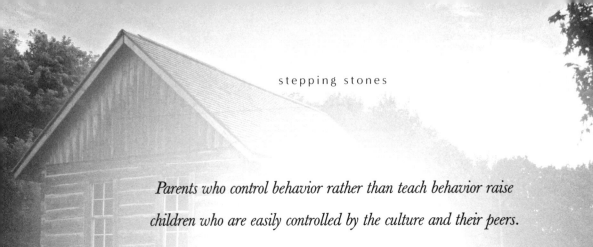

*Parents who control behavior rather than teach behavior raise children who are easily controlled by the culture and their peers.*

⚊⚋⚊

*The principles and behaviors your teen eventually adopts are mostly learned from observing you.*

*The apple doesn't fall far from the tree.*

*Parents of teenagers need to step aside and allow their kids*
*to bend in the winds of life a little more.*

*Parents should begin providing kids with work opportunities*
*and extra doses of freedom and responsibilities.*

*Quit doing everything for your teenagers.*

*It keeps them from developing responsibility and learning*

*self-reliance.*

*When teens begin to experience life,*

*they will make mistakes—lots of them.*

*Your teen is fully capable of remembering what*
*you have asked them to do, the directions you have given,*
*and the rules you have laid down.*

*It takes two to have an argument.*
*Don't be one of them.*

*Growth comes through stress and frustrations,*

*so don't try to eliminate them from your teen's life.*

*Don't try to fix everything.*

*Give your kids a chance to find their own solutions.*

*Talk about and teach what it means to be a good person.*

*Start early.*

———

*Fess up when you blow it. This is the best way*
*to show your teen how and when he or she should apologize.*

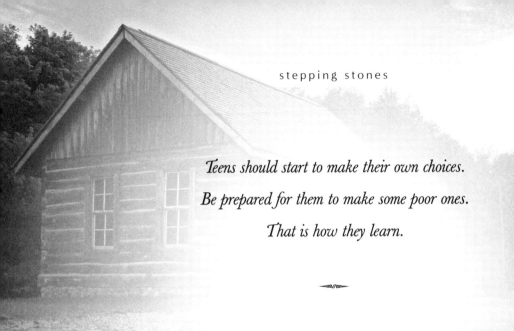

*Teens should start to make their own choices.*

*Be prepared for them to make some poor ones.*

*That is how they learn.*

———

*Share about times when friends have hurt you.*

*It lets your teenager know that he or she is not the only one*

*who has been hurt or betrayed.*

PLANNING

*Build excitement for your teen's future.*

*One of the goals of parenting should be*

*to help teens uncover their talents.*

จ๛

*A teenager's future can be short-circuited by parents*

*who hand him everything on a silver platter.*

*Teaching teens to weigh options and foresee results is*

*a valuable tool they'll use again and again throughout life.*

લ્જ્જ

*Help your teenagers focus on the long-term*

*when setting goals.*

*Are you sabotaging your teenager's future*

*by making success and money her goal?*

༄

*As kids mature in the teen years,*

*they begin searching for the meaning and purpose in life.*

*Be more concerned for the future of kids who do wrong*

*without remorse than of kids who sneak around,*

*then feel guilty about their wrongdoing.*

❧

*Train your teen for the world in which they may eventually live,*

*not just the world in which you hope they will live.*

*Given a little training and a lot of support,*

*most teenagers can far exceed our expectations.*

↻

*Be sure your teen knows that whatever he puts on the internet*

*could affect his future—including college and career.*

*Teenagers actually believe what you say,*
*so be sure what you say builds them up.*

୬୧

*If you are struggling with a difficult teen,*
*remember that God isn't yet finished with her—*
*or you—so don't quit.*

*It is never too late to move from bad decisions*
*to the right direction in life.*

✐

*Nothing matters more than your teen knowing*
*God's purpose for his life.*

*Help your teenager visualize where he wants to be ten years from now. Then help him plan the steps it will take to get there.*

ℐℛ

*Would you rather have a "happy teen" now with no rules and expectations, or a mature and grateful child for the rest of her adult years?*

*Help your teen plan short-term goals (like going camping)*

*and long-term goals (like going to college).*

*It will teach them the skills they need to prepare for the future.*

෮෮

*Parents need to keep their focus on the long term*

*in regard to what they do today to teach their teenager.*

Periodically look at your parenting style and determine
what you need to adjust to fit the age and maturity of your kids.

ↈ

Create excitement for your child's future.
Get them dreaming, planning, and hoping.
Kids with a future act more responsible today.

Shift your parenting style from "providing" your teen
with everything to "preparing" your teen for the next steps in life.

✧

Teens need to become independent. The problem is that often teens
want their freedom too quickly, and parents are often hesitant.

*A parent's goal should be a competent, confident,*

*and self-controlled young adult—not perfection.*

cℓ

*What do you do to ensure your family operates as a family unit,*

*not just several people sleeping under the same roof?*

*Make having fun a priority!*
*To produce a happy teen, be a happy parent.*

ﻬ

*Let your teenagers progress at their own speed,*
*not at your speed.*

126

*Find joy in the fact that your teenager needs you less and less.*

*That's how it is supposed to be.*

ॐ

*Encourage your teen to think BIG!*